D1476887

SPACE EXPLORATION

LIVING IN SPACE

by Philip Wolny

BrightP⬡int Press

San Diego, CA

BrightPoint Press

For more information, contact:
BrightPoint Press
PO Box 27779
San Diego, CA 92198
www.BrightPointPress.com

LIBRARY OF CONGRESS CATALOGING-IN-PUBLICATION DATA

Names: Wolny, Philip, author.
Title: Living in space / by Philip Wolny.
Description: San Diego, CA : BrightPoint Press, [2023] | Series: Space exploration | Includes
    bibliographical references and index. | Audience: Grades 10-12
Identifiers: LCCN 2022003773 (print) | LCCN 2022003774 (eBook) | ISBN 9781678204280
    (hardcover) | ISBN 9781678204297 (eBook)
Subjects: LCSH: International Space Station. | Space stations. | Life support systems (Space
    environment) | Space flight--Physiological effect.
Classification: LCC TL797 .W65 2023 (print) | LCC TL797 (eBook) | DDC 629.44/2--dc23/
    eng/20220216
LC record available at https://lccn.loc.gov/2022003773
LC eBook record available at https://lccn.loc.gov/2022003774

CONTENTS

AT A GLANCE

- Astronauts live onboard the International Space Station (ISS). The ISS is made of many modules that have been added over time.

- Cargo missions carry supplies to the ISS. Supplies include water, air, food, and equipment.

- Future space stations will make use of expandable modules. This will reduce the number of missions needed to build space stations.

- Scientists hope to create rotating space stations in the future. Rotational forces can mimic the effects of gravity.

- Living in space affects the human body. It can damage bones, muscles, and other body parts. It can also affect mental health.

- Scientists work to help astronauts stay healthy while living in space. This will allow astronauts to go on longer missions in the future.

- Exercise is one way astronauts can improve their physical health in space. Artificial gravity on space stations may also have health benefits.

- Scientists hope that space stations will not need to rely on cargo missions in the future. Instead, astronauts will grow their own food. They will recycle 100 percent of their water and air supplies.

INTRODUCTION

LIFE ON THE FINAL FRONTIER

A donut-shaped station lies in deep space. It can **rotate**. It is made up of dozens of connected pods. An astronaut is outside the space station. A tether connects her to the station. It prevents her from drifting off into space. She is on a **space walk** to do repairs.

There is a command center in the middle of the rotating station. Astronauts there check readings on their equipment. They communicate with crew members in other

Space walks usually last between five and eight hours.

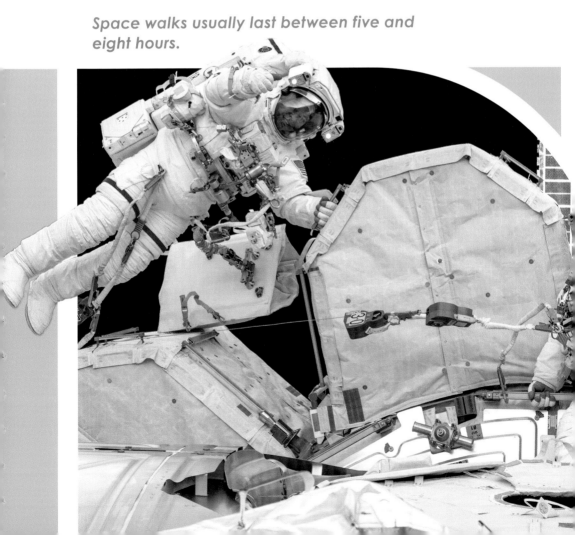

parts of the station. They make sure all the station's systems work properly.

The crew members are excited. The station will get a big delivery today. A cargo ship is arriving with supplies. It carries some items the crew cannot make or grow themselves. Their families have sent them foods from their native countries. There are even rumors about a pizza delivery and sweets like chocolate.

If the cargo mission had been delayed, the astronauts would not have worried. The crew grows food in a large greenhouse. The station recycles air, water, and other

Astronauts will use greenhouses to grow food.

resources the crew needs. Extra supplies sit on loading docks. Smaller spacecraft pick up supplies as they journey to Mars.

THE FUTURE OF LIVING IN SPACE

Scientists hope that people will one day be able to live in space. But there are many challenges to overcome first. The conditions of space can create health challenges. Astronauts need protection from dangers such as **radiation**. They need food, water, and air. Space debris can damage space stations.

New space stations will transform space exploration. Scientists work to create new technologies. Their research will allow humans to go farther in space than ever before. People may even live in space for years at a time.

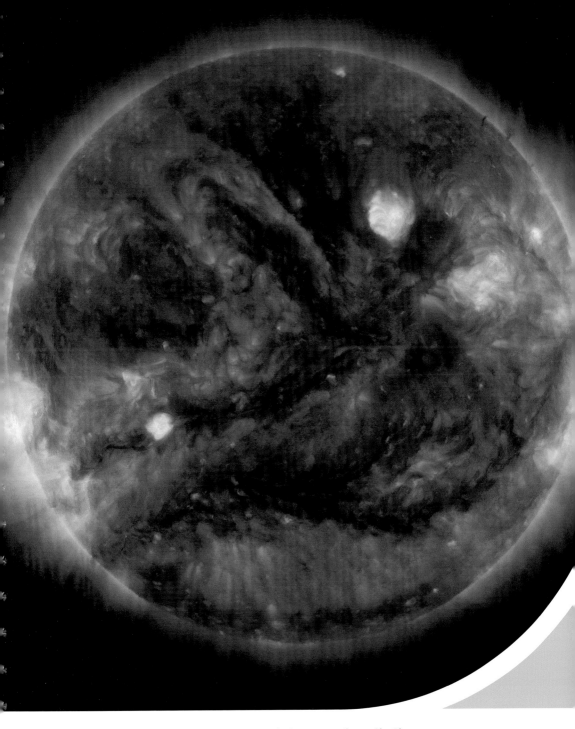

The Sun releases powerful rays of radiation.

1

SPACE STATIONS

On April 12, 1961, Yuri Gagarin flew on the Soviet Union's *Vostok* spacecraft. He completed one **orbit** around Earth. He was the first person to visit space.

The Soviets launched *Salyut* in April 1971. It was the first space station in Earth orbit. The National Aeronautics and Space

Administration (NASA) is the US space agency. NASA launched *Skylab* in May 1973. It was the first US space station.

The Soviet Union dissolved in 1991. Russia carried on the nation's legacy in space. In November, Russia's space program launched Zarya. This **module** was also called the Functional Cargo

A statue in Russia honors Yuri Gagarin's pioneering flight.

Block (FGB). It contained battery power and fuel. The FGB was the first piece of the International Space Station (ISS).

Space programs around the world worked together to build the ISS. NASA launched the Unity module two weeks after the FGB. The space shuttle *Endeavour* carried Unity to orbit. Crew members used the shuttle's robotic arms to connect the modules.

Russia launched Zvezda in July 2000. This module provided air, water, and electricity. It allowed people to live on the station. The first crew members arrived

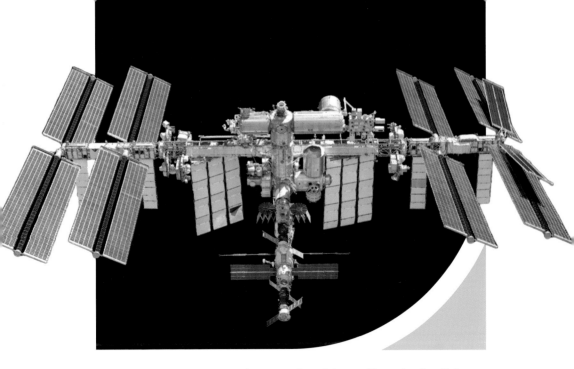

Many space agencies worked together to build the ISS.

in November. Since then, the ISS has been continuously crewed for more than two decades.

It took more than thirty missions to set up the basic parts of the ISS. As of 2021, it is the largest spacecraft ever constructed. New modules were still being added to it.

EXPANDABLE MODULES

Scientists hope to make future modules smaller and lighter. This will make constructing stations much easier. More modules can be sent per launch. It will take fewer launches to build a space station.

Expandable modules are one way to do this. They do not take up as much room on a rocket. They can be expanded after being launched into space.

The Bigelow Expandable Activity Module (BEAM) is being tested on the ISS. It was folded up during launch. It expanded to full

Astronauts posed inside BEAM in 2018.

size after reaching orbit. BEAM is made from lightweight materials like aluminum.

BEAM was installed on the ISS in 2016. NASA planned to test it for only two years. But NASA extended the test in 2017. Jason Crusan works for NASA. He talked about BEAM's success. "It's doing extremely well," Crusan said. "There's really no reason to throw it away."[1]

ARTIFICIAL GRAVITY

People in Earth orbit experience microgravity. This is the state in which people can float around. Earth's gravity still affects them. But in orbit, they are moving so fast that they are constantly in free fall. This creates the effect of weightlessness.

Weightlessness creates many problems for astronauts. The human body evolved in Earth's gravity. It works best under those conditions. Artificial gravity will solve problems related to weightlessness. Gilles Clement researches artificial gravity for

Microgravity allows astronauts to hang upside down in space.

NASA. He says, "We bring food and air.

Why not take gravity with us?"[2]

Engineers are working on spacecraft that

can rotate. Rotational forces can mimic the

effects of gravity. A rotating spacecraft will

be shaped like a wheel or donut. The round

shape provides a consistent rotational force.

This makes artificial gravity even throughout the spacecraft.

A small space station would need to rotate very quickly. Otherwise the rotational force would be too weak to mimic gravity. The speed could give people motion sickness. But building a large space station is challenging. It would take a lot of time and resources to build. It also needs a lot of energy to spin.

Orbital Assembly Corporation (OAC) plans to start building the Voyager Station in 2026. OAC hopes the station will have artificial gravity equal to that of gravity on

THE VOMIT COMET

Astronauts train for weightless conditions. They take flights on special aircraft. These planes make steep climbs and dives. Passengers experience about twenty-five seconds of weightlessness at the top of the climb. Astronauts often get airsick. That is why the planes are nicknamed the Vomit Comet.

the Moon. If successful, the station will be the largest human-made object in space.

New technologies will lower the cost of launching materials into space. Expandable modules will make building space stations more efficient. Artificial gravity will open space travel to more people. People who are not professional astronauts may be able to visit space in the future.

2

A DANGEROUS ENVIRONMENT

The Sun releases radiation that can harm health. Radiation from other stars is also a threat. Radiation can cause skin cancer. It can make people become sick more easily.

Earth's **atmosphere** absorbs much of the Sun's radiation. Astronauts do not have this protection in space. Scientists studied the effects of deep-space radiation in mice. They used a device that fired beams of radiation at the mice. Some mice showed signs of brain damage. People in space may develop similar issues.

Radiation can affect computer systems.

Protection from radiation is necessary to live in space long term. Ruthan Lewis is a NASA engineer. "The space radiation environment will be a critical consideration for everything in the astronauts' daily lives," she said. "You're constantly being bombarded by some amount of radiation."[3]

Equipment onboard the ISS detects radiation levels. It helps keep astronauts safe. Astronauts can take steps to protect themselves when radiation levels are high. They can change course to avoid radiation. They can also move to radiation shelters onboard the spacecraft.

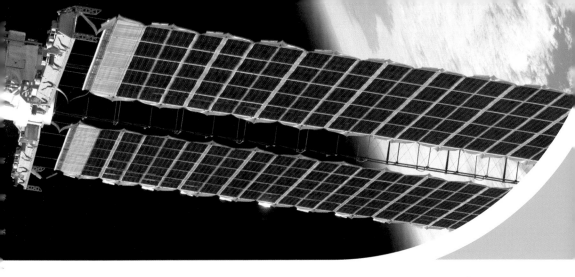

Radiation can damage solar panels on spacecraft.

Building a separate radiation shelter is expensive. It would add weight to the spacecraft. A heavy spacecraft is difficult to launch. Scientists instead figure out ways to use materials already onboard the spacecraft. Any material can create a barrier to protect against radiation.

For example, scientists may store supplies in the walls of the spacecraft.

They may store food and water there.

The thick barrier protects against strong

radiation. The food and water are still safe

to consume. Another idea is to use bodily

waste from astronauts. Waste could be

stored in emptied water bags. The waste

adds a layer of radiation protection.

NASA launched the *Orion* spacecraft in

March 2022. Two dummies were onboard.

They were made to imitate the human body.

The dummies have radiation sensors. One

experiences the full effects of deep-space

radiation. The other wears an AstroRad

radiation vest. The vest is made of materials

that lessen the effects of radiation. It

protects important organs, such as the

lungs and stomach. Scientists will compare

the radiation readings between the two

dummies. They will learn how effective the

AstroRad vest is. This will help them design

protective space suits in the future.

MAGNETIC SHIELDS

NASA has ideas for other forms of radiation shielding. Earth has a magnetic field that blocks much of the Sun's radiation. NASA wonders if it is possible to build a magnetic shield. The shield would deflect radiation.

Space suits protect astronauts from radiation and extreme temperatures.

AIRLESS CONDITIONS

Space is a vacuum. This means there is

no air or air pressure. These conditions are

deadly to an unprotected human. A person

cannot breathe without air. Spacecraft

and space suits protect astronauts. They

provide air to breathe. They are also

pressurized. Their air pressure matches the air pressure on Earth.

There is a difference in air pressure between the inside and outside of a spacecraft. This puts stress on spacecraft. Scientists use strong materials such as aluminum and titanium. These protect the structure of the spacecraft.

SPACE JUNK AND DEBRIS

Space debris can damage a space station. This includes natural and artificial objects. Natural debris includes meteorites and small bits of rock and dust. Artificial

The RemoveDEBRIS satellite launched from the ISS in 2018. It helped test ways to clean up space debris.

debris includes parts of old satellites and spacecraft. These are known as space junk. Pieces of space junk may collide. They may break apart and create even more junk.

The ISS orbits Earth at about 17,000 miles per hour (27,400 kmh). Striking even a small object at this speed could cause damage beyond repair. It could injure or kill an astronaut on a space walk. Former ISS astronaut Scott Kelly talked about never dropping tools on space walks. He said, "If you lose something, not only do you not ever find it again, but it is a piece of orbital debris."[4]

Shields protect the ISS from space debris and junk. Most shields have two or more layers. The bumper is the outermost layer. It takes the full impact of whatever hits it. An object breaks apart when it hits the bumper. The bumper also takes away most of an object's force. Then the lower layers absorb the rest of the force.

The shields become damaged over time. Scientists are working on ways to make shields last longer. They do research to create self-repairing shields. These shields would repair themselves automatically after getting hit. The shields have multiple layers. The outer and inner layers are made of a flexible plastic. A gel separates these layers. The plastic layers can snap back into shape after being struck. The gel reacts to the force and heat of impact. It fills holes if the outer layer is broken.

Scientists also study ways to remove space debris. They want to clean up Earth

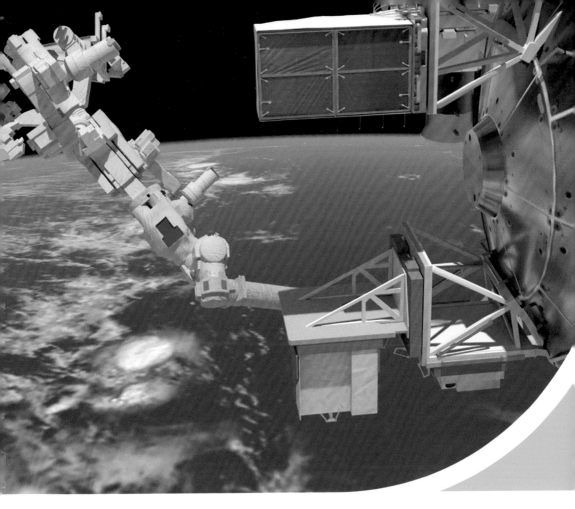

A Space Debris Sensor on the outside of the ISS collects information on space debris.

orbit. A group of scientists is planning to

build a space station called Gateway Earth

by 2050. It will have a facility that can collect

and recycle space junk.

3

BODY AND MIND IN SPACE

Muscles grow bigger and stronger when they are used. They become weak after long periods of inactivity. They also shrink. Some muscles are constantly used on Earth. They work against gravity. For example, muscles in the back and legs hold people upright. Without these muscles, people would fall over.

Microgravity conditions mean these muscles are not being used. Michael Stenger is a NASA scientist. He said, "Being in space is a lot like [lying] around doing nothing."[5]

Being in microgravity affects the way muscles work.

The process of muscle loss can happen quickly. NASA estimates that astronauts can lose up to 20 percent of muscle mass on a spaceflight lasting five to eleven days. The effects may be more severe during longer spaceflights.

The heart pumps blood throughout the body and to the brain. The heart pushes blood upward against the force of gravity. It does not need to work as hard in space. Blood can float easily into the head. Microgravity causes the heart to shrink. Scott Kelly stayed in space for 340 days. Very few astronauts have spent this long in space. His heart lost 27 percent of its mass during this time.

Bone health is also affected by microgravity. Bones support people as they stand and move. They do not need to provide as much support in space. They begin to lose **density**. They become weak. Weak bones are at risk of breaking.

IMPROVING BONE HEALTH

Scientists study ways to improve bone health in space. Nutrients like calcium and vitamin D can strengthen bones. Eating foods with these nutrients helps bone health. NASA is also testing medications. Certain drugs may reduce the risk of broken bones.

Microgravity also causes astronauts' spines to stretch. This puts them at risk for spinal injury. Their spines return to normal when they return to Earth. But the stress on their spines means they remain at high risk for spinal injury.

STAYING FIT AND HEALTHY

Exercise helps astronauts stay healthy in space. It reduces muscle loss. It also protects bone density. Astronauts are required to work out for more than two hours a day. But they still experience muscle loss and reduced bone health.

Astronauts must exercise for more than two hours every day while in space.

These health effects limit the amount of time astronauts can stay in space.

Some forms of exercise are not effective in microgravity conditions. For example, weightlifting would not improve health. There is no gravity to lift against.

Astronauts need special exercise equipment. The Advanced Resistive Exercise Device (ARED) is one example. This device is on the ISS. ARED does not use weights. Instead, astronauts push against resistance. The resistance is created by vacuums in the device. They oppose the astronaut's movements. ARED can be

SKINSUIT

NASA is working on a new tool called Skinsuit. It is wearable. It has many elastic bands. The wearer's movement works against the pressure of the bands. This makes the muscles function as they would in regular gravity conditions. Engineers believe the Skinsuit could help prevent astronauts' spines from stretching.

adjusted to up to 600 pounds (272 kg) of resistance. The ISS also has a treadmill and exercise bike.

The exercise equipment on the ISS weighs about 4,000 pounds (1,800 kg). Heavy equipment is expensive to launch. It also takes up a lot of room. Scientists have developed smaller exercise equipment for future missions. One example is the Resistive Overload Combined with Kinetic Yo-Yo (ROCKY) device. ROCKY weighs just 20 pounds (9 kg). It uses resistance for strength training. ROCKY works like a rowing machine.

Astronauts must work, sleep, and eat in close quarters for long periods of time.

MENTAL HEALTH

Living in space can affect mental health.

Astronauts on the ISS have stressful

schedules. Astronauts must always be alert.

Mistakes made in space could be deadly.

Spacecraft are often small. Astronauts

have little privacy. This can cause conflict

among the crew. Astronauts need to work together to survive the dangers of space. Conflict may occur more often on longer missions. **Isolation** can cause mental health problems. Astronauts may spend a lot of time together. But they also spend months away from friends and family. This can lead to depression and anxiety. Relatives and friends can send presents and letters during resupply launches.

Astronauts in Earth orbit can video chat with family. Communication happens almost instantly. But communication delays will occur during deep-space missions.

Astronauts on these missions will not have real-time contact with family. This can harm mental health.

Astronauts on the ISS have a view of Earth. It can make being away from home less painful. Deep-space missions will not have this view. Nicole Stott is a retired astronaut. She said, "Think about it. Nine months on a relatively small spaceship to go to Mars. At some point, you don't have that stunning view of Earth out the window anymore."[6]

Virtual reality (VR) systems may help reduce stress. Six scientists on Earth tested

Virtual reality may be useful to help mental health in space.

the VR technology. They lived together in

isolation for a year. This mimics the isolation

during long space missions. The scientists

used VR to visit museums and beaches.

NASA believes VR will be useful. The

technology could help crews feel connected

to Earth during long missions.

4

SPACE LOGISTICS AND LIFE SUPPORT

Cargo missions to the ISS happen about every sixty to ninety days. A Russian cargo mission in 2016 carried 2.6 tons (2.4 metric tons) of cargo. This included fuel, water, and oxygen for the station. A US cargo mission in late 2021 delivered science equipment, space walking gear, and computers. It also carried Christmas

presents from the astronauts' families.

There are usually six crew members on

the ISS at any given time. Everything they

need must be requested weeks or months

Rockets launch thousands of pounds of cargo for the ISS.

Astronauts need a water supply to live in space for long periods of time.

in advance. The main supplies are food, water, and oxygen. Cargo missions also carry other essentials. Spacecraft bring up fresh clothing. Astronauts need supplies for science experiments. Returning cargo ships take back things that need repairs.

SELF-SUSTAINING IN SPACE

It takes cargo spacecraft hours to travel to the ISS. Cargo missions to deep space will take months. Mission planners must figure out how to carry large amounts of food. They must also figure out ways to fully recycle water and air.

NASA hopes that missions in the future will not need resupply visits. They would be self-contained missions. New technologies are needed to make missions fully sustainable.

The ISS relies on cargo missions. But it recycles much of its water and oxygen.

Two systems work together to make this happen. One is the water recovery system (WRS). The other is the oxygen generation system (OGS). Solar panels help power these systems.

The WRS takes in water from many sources on the ISS. It collects moisture from the air. It also takes in water that has been used for bathing. It even collects the astronauts' urine. The urine is filtered and purified. It becomes clean water that can be used again. Astronaut Douglas Wheelock has joked about water recycling, saying, "Yesterday's coffee is tomorrow's coffee."[7]

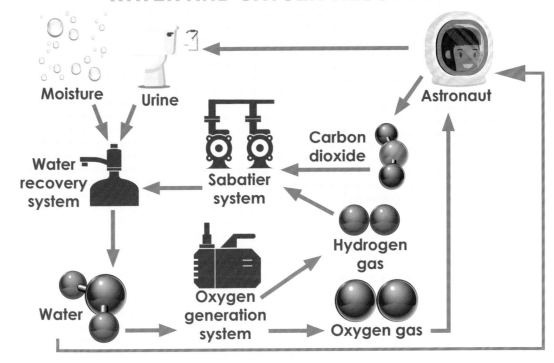

Systems onboard the ISS help recycle oxygen and water. The Sabatier system helps produce water.

Water is also needed for the OGS.

Water contains the elements oxygen and

hydrogen. Special electrical devices split

the water into these parts. Oxygen and

hydrogen become gases after being split

apart. Astronauts breathe the oxygen.

Astronauts breathe out carbon dioxide. This gas has oxygen atoms. It is fed into the Sabatier system along with the hydrogen gas from the OGS. The Sabatier system combines hydrogen with oxygen atoms. This produces more water. The water is then collected by the WRS.

SELF-CONTAINED MISSIONS

Long trips will require a lot of food. The food has to keep for a long time. Scientists remove water from some foods. This reduces their weight. It also prevents them from spoiling. One example is milk and cereal. These are packaged together. But the milk is dry. Astronauts must add water before eating. They also add water to the soups they eat.

Scientists hope that astronauts will be able to grow their own food in space. Some crops have been grown on the ISS. Astronauts have grown several kinds of

NO CRUMBS

Some food items are dangerous in microgravity conditions. They produce a lot of crumbs. The crumbs float around. They can damage space equipment. They can also get into astronauts' eyes. This is why bread is banned from space missions. Salt, pepper, and other spices are stored in liquid form.

lettuce. They have also grown kale, wheat, and other crops. Pea pods were the first fruit to be grown in space. Fruits are the parts of a plant that contain seeds. A 2021 NASA experiment grew red and green chili peppers.

Fruits and vegetables have different nutrients. A wide selection of both improves health. NASA's Ray Wheeler says that growing food has many benefits. Freshly grown foods can remind astronauts of home. "Having fresh food like these available in space could have a positive impact on people's moods," he said.[8]

An astronaut tends to chili pepper plants growing on the ISS.

It will take a long time before astronauts can grow all the food they need. They will need large gardens or greenhouses.

They also need advanced sensors and other instruments. Sensors track plant growth. They make sure food is grown efficiently. Data from the sensors can help scientists improve growing methods.

The knowledge scientists have gained on the ISS is just the beginning. Scientists

SPACE SALAD

In 2015, ISS astronauts ate a vegetable grown in space for the first time. Scott Kelly was one of the astronauts who tried the red romaine lettuce grown aboard the station. Kelly said, "Tastes good, kind of like arugula."

Quoted in Alyssa Newcomb, "Lettuce Feast: Astronauts Get First Taste of Veggies Harvested in Space," ABC News, August 10, 2015. https://abcnews.go.com.

New technologies must be developed before people are able to live in space for long periods of time.

develop new technologies. They learn how

to protect humans during long missions.

They make plans to send people to

deep space. In the future, living in space

permanently may be a reality.

GLOSSARY

atmosphere

the layer of gas surrounding a planet or moon

density

the amount of material in a given amount of space

isolation

the state of being alone or feeling separated from other people

module

a unit that is operational on its own but can also be part of the larger structure of a space station

orbit

a round path that an object takes when traveling around another object in space

radiation

a form of energy that can cause health problems

rotate

to spin around a center line

space walk

a time when an astronaut is in space outside of a spacecraft or space station

SOURCE NOTES

CHAPTER ONE: SPACE STATIONS

1. Quoted in Joe Palca, "After a Year in Space, the Air Hasn't Gone Out of NASA's Inflated Module," *NPR*, July 26, 2017. www.npr.org.

2. Quoted in Adam Hadhazy, "Artificial Gravity's Attraction," *Aerospace America*, April 2017. https://aerospaceamerica.aiaa.org.

CHAPTER TWO: A DANGEROUS ENVIRONMENT

3. Quoted in Sarah Frazier, "Real Martians: How to Protect Astronauts from Space Radiation on Mars," *NASA*, September 30, 2015. www.nasa.gov.

4. Quoted in David Plotz, "Exit Interview: Scott Kelly, an Astronaut Who Spent a Year in Space," *Atlas Obscura*, November 9, 2017. www.atlasobscura.com.

CHAPTER THREE: BODY AND MIND IN SPACE

5. Quoted in Sarah Scoles, "Astronaut Gear of the Future May Fight Bone and Muscle Loss," *Wired*, November 9, 2021. www.wired.com.

6. Quoted in Alex Lin, "The Complex Relationship Between Mental Health and Space Travel," *Supercluster*, May 28, 2019. www.supercluster.com.

CHAPTER FOUR: SPACE LOGISTICS AND LIFE SUPPORT

7. Quoted in Michael J. I. Brown, "Curious Kids: Where Does the Oxygen Come from in the International Space Station, and Why Don't They Run Out of Air?" *Conversation*, December 5, 2017. https://theconversation.com.

8. Quoted in Linda Herridge, "Meals Ready to Eat: Expedition 44 Crew Members Sample Leafy Greens Grown on Space Station," *NASA*, August 7, 2015. www.nasa.gov.

FOR FURTHER RESEARCH

BOOKS

Tammy Gagne, *Colonizing Mars*. San Diego, CA: BrightPoint Press, 2023.

Christa C. Hogan, *Space Stations*. New York: Weigl, 2020.

Elsie Olson, *Spectacular Space Stations*. Minneapolis, MN: Lerner, 2019.

INTERNET SOURCES

Hannah Devlin, "Space-Grown Lettuce to Give Astronauts a More Varied Diet," *Guardian*, March 6, 2020. www.theguardian.com.

Alice Gorman and Justin St. P. Walsh, "How to Live in Space: What We've Learned from Twenty Years of the International Space Station," *Conversation*, November 1, 2020. https://theconversation.com.

Elizabeth Howell, "Scott Kelly: The American Astronaut Who Spent a Year in Space," *Space*, September 4, 2019. www.space.com.

Coalition for Deep Space Exploration
https://exploredeepspace.com

The Coalition for Deep Space Exploration is an association of more than fifty businesses and organizations working to ensure US leadership in space exploration.

ISS National Laboratory
www.issnationallab.org

The International Space Station's National Laboratory is a one-stop online resource discussing the history and current projects of the ISS.

National Aeronautics and Space Administration (NASA)
www.nasa.gov

NASA.gov is the main internet portal for the US space agency NASA. It is the main stakeholder in the International Space Station.

INDEX

IMAGE CREDITS

ABOUT THE AUTHOR

Philip Wolny is a writer and editor who was born in Bydgoszcz, Poland, and raised in Queens, New York. He currently resides in Florida with his wife and daughter. He and his family sometimes marvel at the rockets launching from the nearby Space Coast.